W9-ARL-755

Dear Reader:

The book you are about to read is the latest bestseller from the St. Martin's True Crime Library, the imprint *The New York Times* calls "the leader in true crime!" The True Crime Library offers you fascinating accounts of the latest, most sensational crimes that have captured the national attention. St. Martin's is the publisher of John Glatt's riveting and horrifying SECRETS IN THE CELLAR, which shines a light on the man who shocked the world when it was revealed that he had kept his daughter locked in his hidden basement for 24 years. In the Edgar-nominated WRITTEN IN BLOOD, Diane Fanning looks at Michael Petersen, a Marine-turned-novelist found guilty of beating his wife to death and pushing her down the stairs of their home—only to reveal another similar death from his past. In the book you now hold, SEE HOW MUCH YOU LOVE ME, Amber Hunt explores the case of a troubled teenager and the brutal deaths of his parents.

St. Martin's True Crime Library gives you the stories behind the headlines. Our authors take you right to the scene of the crime and into the minds of the most notorious murderers to show you what really makes them tick. St. Martin's True Crime Library paperbacks are better than the most terrifying thriller, because it's all true! The next time you want a crackling good read, make sure it's got the St. Martin's True Crime Library logo on the spine—you'll be up all night!

Charles E. Spicer

Charles E. Spicer, Jr.
Executive Editor, St. Martin's True Crime Library

TITLES BY AMBER HUNT

Dead but Not Forgotten
All-American Murder
See How Much You Love Me

From the True Crime Library of
St. Martin's Paperbacks

SEE HOW MUCH YOU LOVE ME

AMBER HUNT

St. Martin's Paperbacks

NOTE: If you purchased this book without a cover you should be aware that this book is stolen property. It was reported as "unsold and destroyed" to the publisher, and neither the author nor the publisher has received any payment for this "stripped book."

SEE HOW MUCH YOU LOVE ME

Copyright © 2014 by Amber Hunt.

All rights reserved.

For information address St. Martin's Press, 175 Fifth Avenue, New York, NY 10010.

EAN: 978-1-250-01035-3

Printed in the United States of America

St. Martin's Paperbacks edition / June 2014

St. Martin's Paperbacks are published by St. Martin's Press, 175 Fifth Avenue, New York, NY 10010.

10 9 8 7 6 5 4 3 2 1

To the countless nameless victims of crime, caught in the ripple effects of others' unthinkably selfish deeds.

CHAPTER 1

He stood behind her, a hammer clenched in his hand. He was silent, and she was oblivious. The hammer's handle was smooth in his palm. He stared at her as she typed absentmindedly on the family computer. He was still for a long time and he held the hammer at his side as he eyed his mother's head.

Mary Jo Hadley sat in a bluish gray, cloth-covered desk chair, staring at the computer monitor. It was an awkward place for a computer, right in the middle of the kitchen. It was housed in a cheaply made computer desk—a birch-colored fake-wood number that didn't match the room's other wooden furniture. But then nothing really matched in this house. A china hutch to the left of the computer desk was a mahogany-stained wood— real wood—that was pretty close in color to a trunk the family used as a coffee table on the other side of the combined kitchen and living room setup. Like a lot of Florida homes, the Hadleys' featured a great room in addition to a more formal sitting room, and the floor was an off-white tile, a material that helped keep the great room cool and, in theory, was easy to clean. In reality, it often wasn't clean. The tile grout had darkened over the years, and no amount of scrubbing ever got that floor completely sparkling anymore.

Near the coffee table trunk was a dresser far lighter in color, almost yellow in fact, and pastel-colored clothes peeked out of a top drawer. Across the room, the kitchen boasted dark cabinets, cheap ones, like the kind you'd expect to see in a mid-range apartment. The appliances were out of date and a little dirty. It's not how Mary Jo had necessarily envisioned the house when she and her husband moved in twenty-five years ago, but it'd been through a lot, serving as home first to the young couple, and then to two boys as they grew and grew and grew. Ryan, the older, had just moved out a month or so ago. Tyler was six months shy of eighteen, almost a man now. Not that he was acting like a man yet. In fact, in the past year Tyler had become quite a handful. He'd always had a bit of a dark side, a melancholy undercurrent that would come and go. But lately, it was coming more often than going. He'd even begun saying lately that he wanted to kill himself. That tore at Mary Jo's heart, and she'd searched on the family computer for therapy in which she could enroll her once towheaded boy. At seventeen, though, he wasn't towheaded anymore. He was six foot one and awkward and he had his mother's eyes.

And now he was standing behind her with a hammer in his hand.

* * *

A few blocks away, Daniel Roberts was catching his breath. He'd been running away from the Hadley home, though he wasn't entirely sure why. He'd stopped by to visit with his friend Michael Mandell. Michael was Danny's best friend, and Tyler was Michael's best friend, so even though Danny wasn't as crazy about Tyler as Michael was, the three hung out together about once a week. They'd drive around, hang out with Michael's girlfriend, smoke a little weed. Michael didn't drink, but Tyler and Danny did, so sometimes they drank together. Typical bored, rebel-without-a-cause teenage stuff.

This visit started out weird and just got weirder. Danny had ended up getting stuck at Tyler's after Michael's battery died and he couldn't give him a lift back. It was a little awkward—it was Danny's first time even being at Tyler's house, after all—and Tyler's folks weren't home. He'd heard such awful things about Tyler's parents, too. That his mom never let him leave the house. That his dad beat on him regularly. He couldn't count how many times Tyler joked about killing them. As Michael left the house with his father, who'd swung by to pick him up, leaving Danny behind to potentially meet the infamous parents, he snuck in a word with Michael. He didn't want to be there, man. Tyler's folks were such assholes.

They're not so bad, Michael assured him. Tyler makes them sound like they're horrible, but they're nice. Just chill out and when they come home, say you walked all the way here and just wanted to hang out with Tyler.

Danny felt better. He'd try to get Tyler to drive him home, but if the folks came home first, he'd just explain that he was there to hang out. No big deal. Maybe they were regular parents after all. Tyler always did sound like he was joking when he said he hated them. Sure, the jokes got a little pointed, like the other day when Tyler said he'd bought the pickaxe and had come so close—*so close*—to killing them. That kid had a twisted sense of humor.

So Danny made chitchat and sized up the home.

"Hey, it's really nice here," he told Tyler.

Tyler scoffed. "This isn't nice. *Your* house is nice."

Danny wasn't sure why the reaction. He looked around. The place wasn't a dump. There was obviously plenty of food. Paintings and photos hung on the walls. The fireplace in the great room was a nice touch, too. Maybe it was because he'd envisioned Tyler living in more of a prison than a home, but the place was surprisingly normal. Hell, there was even a screened-in pool in the backyard. Sure, it was nice.

"You're lucky. You have your own laptop," Danny tried again.

"No, no." Tyler shrugged him off.

A few minutes passed. It was still kind of uncomfortable. He wanted Tyler to just drive him home. That was another thing—Tyler had a car. He had a car, and he always had money—like, *lots* of money, sometimes six or seven hundred-dollar bills in his wallet. Tyler maybe didn't have it as bad as he'd made it sound all these years. Danny decided to ask for that lift, but just as he started the sentence, he noticed an SUV pulling into the driveway. For a split second, he and Tyler froze. Then Tyler's reaction was swift and surprising.

"Run, run, run, go, go, go!" Tyler shouted, and the two teens bolted toward the back door. Danny slammed into a watercooler, knocking it over. He slammed into other stuff, too, but couldn't tell what he was hitting in his rush. Tyler was right with him, running him toward a fence in the backyard. Tyler offered him a boost and Danny scurried over, landing on the other side with a thud. And then he kept running.

He didn't know why he was running, though. He'd expected to meet the parents; he'd mentally prepared for it. Why the jolt of panic from Tyler? Were they really so awful that even seeing Danny in the house would've caused them to blow a fuse? Maybe it had to do with the party Tyler was planning later that night. He'd told Michael and him about it earlier, and he'd posted about it on his Facebook page: "party at my crib tonight," he'd written, "maybe." He'd first posted it at 1:15 p.m. His parents probably didn't know about the party, so maybe that's why Tyler had rushed him out the door. Danny didn't know the answer. Eventually, he did what most people do when they're running for no reason in the July Florida heat: He stopped. He called a buddy and asked for a lift. *Dammit.* He realized he'd left his cell phone charger at Tyler's house. It'd been in his pocket. For some reason, he'd set it on the counter next to Tyler's laptop. In the unexpected rush, he'd forgotten to grab it.

No worries, though. Tyler was going to have that party. They'd all meet up again at the party.

Word about Tyler's party had started spreading immediately. Tyler hadn't had many parties before, maybe one or two a year when his folks were out of town. His friends knew his parents didn't let him out much. Some had heard horror stories. Tyler's dad was a big man, tall and very heavy, about three hundred pounds. Word among the kids was that his dad—Blake was his name—would sometimes clock Tyler for no good reason.

"He always looks like he'd been punched in the face," Danny would later tell a detective.

Danny and the other kids didn't know what many people knew about Blake—that he was a gentle giant who actually ticked his wife off now and then for being too lenient with the boys. He had a hard time with discipline. Just wasn't in his nature to punish his sons. But because the kids who knew Tyler didn't know this, and because Tyler told them he was punched, they believed he was punched. *What a rough life Tyler must lead,* they thought. *Parents can be so cruel sometimes.* So they figured that when Tyler's party messages went out, his parents must be out of town. Those ogres would never let him have a party. And good for Tyler to take advantage of it. The responses to the Facebook message started accumulating. Friends of friends got text messages with the address. Tyler posted a cell phone number that his closest friends recognized was his dad's. His parents had confiscated his own phone after catching him drunk recently, so Tyler couldn't post his own digits. This was going to be an amazing party.

But first, Tyler had to get ready.

He'd been standing behind his mother for five minutes, hammer in hand, before he finally struck a blow.